THIS MAP BELONGS TO...

_____

Welcome!

Welcome to your empowering Daily Success Map! This planner and journal is designed to help you navigate each day with authenticity and confidence. It provides inspiration, guidance, and practical strategies to conquer your goals and embrace your true self. The mission is to support self-discovery, growth, and empowerment, guiding you towards a life filled with purpose, fulfillment, and unwavering confidence. By using this planner, you are nurturing your authentic self and taking a powerful step towards building confidence from within.

Let the journey begin!

Hayley:
Creator of the Daily Success Map,
Author, Coach, Wife.

Mindset & Expectations

Embracing an abundant confident mindset is the key to unlocking your full potential and living a life of authentic confidence.

This mindset is grounded in self-acceptance, self-love, and a deep understanding of your unique strengths and capabilities.

It is about acknowledging your worth and shifting your focus from self-doubt to gratitude and abundance.

Trust in your journey, celebrate your unique qualities, and approach each day with confidence.

How To: Guide & Tips

Identify Goals That Matter:

Take the time to reflect on your aspirations and identify the goals that truly matter to you. Consider your long-term vision and break it down into smaller, actionable goals that align with your values and passions.

Set Monthly Intentions:

At the start of each month, set clear intentions for what you want to accomplish. These intentions act as guide-posts, helping you stay focused and motivated throughout the month. Keep them visible as a reminder for your goals.

Establish a Good Routine:

Create a routine that supports your goals and includes activities such as habit building, self-care, exercise, and focused work time. Dedicate specific time slots for each activity, allowing for a balanced and fulfilling day and week.

   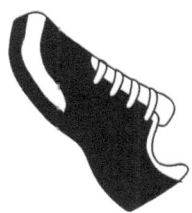

Shade The Objects To Be Accountible.

How To: Guide & Tips

Create Action Plans:
Break down your goals into actionable steps by creating detailed action plans. Identify the specific tasks, deadlines, and resources required to achieve each goal.

Set Daily Intentions:
Set daily intentions that align with your monthly goals and overall vision. These intentions can be specific actions, attitudes, or qualities you want to embody throughout the day.

Reflection:
Take time to reflect on your progress, challenges, and achievements. Use the reflection pages to jot down insights, lessons learned, and areas for improvement.

Celebrations:
Acknowledge and celebrate your successes, no matter how big or small. Take time to appreciate your achievements and milestones along the way. Use the celebration pages in the planner to record your accomplishments and express gratitude for your journey.

Four Goals I Intend To Achieve By The End Of This Map!

01

I Will Accomplish This By-

02

I Will Accomplish This By-

03

I Will Accomplish This By-

04

I Will Accomplish This By-

> *Your Journey To Success Begins With A Single Step Towards Your Dreams.*

MONTH: _____

AIM FOR
THIS HALF

YEAR: _____

AIM FOR
THIS HALF

> *Embrace The Challenges, For They Are The Stepping Stones To Your Greatness*

WEEKLY LIST

INTENTION FOR THE WEEK OF:
_____

MONDAY	TUESDAY

WEDNESDAY	THURSDAY

FRIDAY	SATURDAY
	SUNDAY

PRIORITIES

_____
_____
_____
_____
_____
_____
_____
_____
_____
_____
_____
_____
_____
_____
_____
_____
_____
_____
_____
_____
_____
_____

TO DO LIST

WEEK | | |

PRIORITIES

- [ ] _____
- [ ] _____
- [ ] _____

TASKS

- [ ] _____
- [ ] _____
- [ ] _____
- [ ] _____
- [ ] _____
- [ ] _____
- [ ] _____
- [ ] _____

SELF CARE

- [ ] _____
- [ ] _____
- [ ] _____

Affirmation Of The Week

I Acknowledge And Celebrate All The Victories, Big And Small, That I Achieved This Week.

TAKEAWAY

WEEKLY LIST

INTENTION FOR THE WEEK OF:
_____

MONDAY

TUESDAY

WEDNESDAY

THURSDAY

FRIDAY

SATURDAY

SUNDAY

PRIORITIES

_____
_____
_____
_____
_____
_____
_____
_____
_____
_____
_____
_____
_____
_____
_____
_____
_____
_____
_____
_____
_____
_____
_____
_____
_____

TO DO LIST

WEEK | | | |

PRIORITIES

- [ ] _____
- [ ] _____
- [ ] _____

TASKS

- [ ] _____
- [ ] _____
- [ ] _____
- [ ] _____
- [ ] _____
- [ ] _____
- [ ] _____
- [ ] _____

SELF CARE

- [ ] _____
- [ ] _____
- [ ] _____

Affirmation Of The Week

I Am Grateful For All The Positive Experiences And Blessings That Came My Way This Week.

TAKEAWAY

WEEKLY LIST

INTENTION FOR THE WEEK OF:
_____

MONDAY

TUESDAY

WEDNESDAY

THURSDAY

FRIDAY

SATURDAY

SUNDAY

PRIORITIES

_____
_____
_____
_____
_____
_____
_____
_____
_____
_____
_____
_____
_____
_____
_____
_____
_____
_____
_____
_____
_____
_____
_____
_____
_____

TO DO LIST

WEEK | | |

PRIORITIES

- [ ] _____
- [ ] _____
- [ ] _____

TASKS

- [ ] _____
- [ ] _____
- [ ] _____
- [ ] _____
- [ ] _____
- [ ] _____
- [ ] _____
- [ ] _____

SELF CARE

- [ ] _____
- [ ] _____
- [ ] _____

Affirmation Of The Week

I Release Negativity Or Disappointments From This Week And Embrace A Fresh Start.

TAKEAWAY

WEEKLY LIST

INTENTION FOR THE WEEK OF:
_____

MONDAY

TUESDAY

WEDNESDAY

THURSDAY

FRIDAY

SATURDAY

SUNDAY

PRIORITIES

TO DO LIST

WEEK | | |

PRIORITIES

- [ ] _____
- [ ] _____
- [ ] _____

TASKS

- [ ] _____
- [ ] _____
- [ ] _____
- [ ] _____
- [ ] _____
- [ ] _____
- [ ] _____
- [ ] _____

SELF CARE

- [ ] _____
- [ ] _____
- [ ] _____

Affirmation Of The Week

I Am Proud Of Myself For The Progress I Made Towards My Goals This Week.

TAKEAWAY

HABIT TRACKER

HABIT:
_____

TAKEAWAY

☐ _____

☐ _____

☐ _____

☐ _____

MONTHLY CHECK IN

I WAS AUTHENTIC THIS MONTH

I WAS CONFIDENT THIS MONTH

I WAS HUMBLE THIS MONTH

I WAS MY BEST THIS MONTH

Remember To Embrace Yourself, In Humility And Victories!

THIS MONTH WAS...

- [ ] _____
- [ ] _____
- [ ] _____
- [ ] _____
- [ ] _____
- [ ] _____
- [ ] _____
- [ ] _____
- [ ] _____

TAKEAWAY

MONTH: _____

AIM FOR
THIS HALF

YEAR: _____

AIM FOR THIS HALF

> *Dare To Dream Big, And Let Your Actions Speak Louder Than Your Doubts.*

WEEKLY LIST

INTENTION FOR THE WEEK OF:
_____

MONDAY

TUESDAY

WEDNESDAY

THURSDAY

FRIDAY

SATURDAY

SUNDAY

PRIORITIES

TO DO LIST

WEEK | | | |

PRIORITIES

- [ ] _____
- [ ] _____
- [ ] _____

TASKS

- [ ] _____
- [ ] _____
- [ ] _____
- [ ] _____
- [ ] _____
- [ ] _____
- [ ] _____
- [ ] _____

SELF CARE

- [ ] _____
- [ ] _____
- [ ] _____

Affirmation Of The Week

I Choose To Focus On The Lessons Learned And Growth Achieved Throughout This Week.

TAKEAWAY

WEEKLY LIST

INTENTION FOR THE WEEK OF:
_____

MONDAY

TUESDAY

WEDNESDAY

THURSDAY

FRIDAY

SATURDAY

SUNDAY

PRIORITIES

TO DO LIST

WEK | | | |

PRIORITIES

- [ ] _____
- [ ] _____
- [ ] _____

TASKS

- [ ] _____
- [ ] _____
- [ ] _____
- [ ] _____
- [ ] _____
- [ ] _____
- [ ] _____
- [ ] _____

SELF CARE

- [ ] _____
- [ ] _____
- [ ] _____

Affirmation Of The Week

I Am Thankful For The Opportunities That Presented Themselves To Me This Week.

TAKEAWAY

WEEKLY LIST

INTENTION FOR THE WEEK OF:
_____

MONDAY

TUESDAY

WEDNESDAY

THURSDAY

FRIDAY

SATURDAY

SUNDAY

PRIORITIES

_____
_____
_____
_____
_____
_____
_____
_____
_____
_____
_____
_____
_____
_____
_____
_____
_____
_____
_____
_____
_____
_____
_____
_____
_____

TO DO LIST

WEEK | | |

PRIORITIES

- [ ] _____
- [ ] _____
- [ ] _____

TASKS

- [ ] _____
- [ ] _____
- [ ] _____
- [ ] _____
- [ ] _____
- [ ] _____
- [ ] _____
- [ ] _____

SELF CARE

- [ ] _____
- [ ] _____
- [ ] _____

Affirmation Of The Week

I Am Deserving Of Rest, Rejuvenation, And Self-care To Recharge For The Next Week.

TAKEAWAY

WEEKLY LIST

INTENTION FOR THE WEEK OF:
_____

MONDAY

TUESDAY

PRIORITIES

WEDNESDAY

THURSDAY

FRIDAY

SATURDAY

SUNDAY

TO DO LIST

WEEK | | |

PRIORITIES

- [ ] _____
- [ ] _____
- [ ] _____

TASKS

- [ ] _____
- [ ] _____
- [ ] _____
- [ ] _____
- [ ] _____
- [ ] _____
- [ ] _____
- [ ] _____

SELF CARE

- [ ] _____
- [ ] _____
- [ ] _____

Affirmation Of The Week

I Am Confident In My Abilities To Overcome Any Challenges That Come My Way.

TAKEAWAY

HABIT TRACKER

HABIT:
_____

TAKEAWAY

- ☐ _____
- ☐ _____
- ☐ _____
- ☐ _____

MONTHLY CHECK IN

I WAS AUTHENTIC THIS MONTH

I WAS CONFIDENT THIS MONTH

I WAS HUMBLE THIS MONTH

I WAS MY BEST THIS MONTH

Remember To Embrace Yourself, In Humility And Victories!

THIS MONTH WAS...

- [ ] _____
- [ ] _____
- [ ] _____
- [ ] _____
- [ ] _____
- [ ] _____
- [ ] _____
- [ ] _____
- [ ] _____

TAKEAWAY

MONTH: _____

**AIM FOR
THIS HALF**

YEAR: _____

AIM FOR THIS HALF

> *The Key To Success Is Not Found In Luck, But In The Unwavering Belief In Yourself.*

WEEKLY LIST

INTENTION FOR THE WEEK OF:
_____

MONDAY	TUESDAY

WEDNESDAY	THURSDAY

FRIDAY	SATURDAY
	SUNDAY

PRIORITIES

_____
_____
_____
_____
_____
_____
_____
_____
_____
_____
_____
_____
_____
_____
_____
_____
_____
_____
_____
_____
_____
_____
_____
_____

TO DO LIST

WEK | | | |

PRIORITIES

- [ ] _____
- [ ] _____
- [ ] _____

TASKS

- [ ] _____
- [ ] _____
- [ ] _____
- [ ] _____
- [ ] _____
- [ ] _____
- [ ] _____
- [ ] _____

SELF CARE

- [ ] _____
- [ ] _____
- [ ] _____

Affirmation Of The Week

I Release Any Self-doubt Or Criticism And Embrace Self-compassion And Self-love.

TAKEAWAY

WEEKLY LIST

INTENTION FOR THE WEEK OF:
_____

MONDAY

TUESDAY

PRIORITIES

_____
_____
_____
_____
_____
_____
_____
_____

WEDNESDAY

THURSDAY

_____
_____
_____
_____
_____
_____
_____
_____
_____
_____
_____

FRIDAY

SATURDAY

_____
_____
_____
_____

SUNDAY

_____
_____
_____

TO DO LIST

WEEK | | | |

PRIORITIES

- [ ] _____
- [ ] _____
- [ ] _____

TASKS

- [ ] _____
- [ ] _____
- [ ] _____
- [ ] _____
- [ ] _____
- [ ] _____
- [ ] _____
- [ ] _____

SELF CARE

- [ ] _____
- [ ] _____
- [ ] _____

Affirmation Of The Week

I Am Excited And Open To The Possibilities And Opportunities That The Next Week Holds.

TAKEAWAY

WEEKLY LIST

INTENTION FOR THE WEEK OF:
_____

MONDAY

TUESDAY

WEDNESDAY

THURSDAY

FRIDAY

SATURDAY

SUNDAY

PRIORITIES

_____
_____
_____
_____
_____
_____
_____
_____
_____
_____
_____
_____
_____
_____
_____
_____
_____
_____
_____
_____
_____
_____
_____
_____
_____
_____
_____

TO DO LIST

WEEK | | |

PRIORITIES

- [ ] _____
- [ ] _____
- [ ] _____

TASKS

- [ ] _____
- [ ] _____
- [ ] _____
- [ ] _____
- [ ] _____
- [ ] _____
- [ ] _____
- [ ] _____

SELF CARE

- [ ] _____
- [ ] _____
- [ ] _____

Affirmation Of The Week

I Am Grateful For The Support And Encouragement I Received From Loved Ones This Week.

TAKEAWAY

WEEKLY LIST

INTENTION FOR THE WEEK OF:
_____

MONDAY

TUESDAY

WEDNESDAY

THURSDAY

FRIDAY

SATURDAY

SUNDAY

PRIORITIES

_____
_____
_____
_____
_____
_____
_____
_____
_____
_____
_____
_____
_____
_____
_____
_____
_____
_____
_____
_____
_____
_____
_____
_____
_____

TO DO LIST

WEEK | | |

PRIORITIES

- [ ] _____
- [ ] _____
- [ ] _____

TASKS

- [ ] _____
- [ ] _____
- [ ] _____
- [ ] _____
- [ ] _____
- [ ] _____
- [ ] _____
- [ ] _____

SELF CARE

- [ ] _____
- [ ] _____
- [ ] _____

Affirmation Of The Week

I Choose To See Setbacks As Stepping Stones Towards Greater Success.

TAKEAWAY

HABIT TRACKER

HABIT:
_____

TAKEAWAY

- ☐ _____
- ☐ _____
- ☐ _____
- ☐ _____

MONTHLY CHECK IN

I WAS AUTHENTIC THIS MONTH

I WAS CONFIDENT THIS MONTH

I WAS HUMBLE THIS MONTH

I WAS MY BEST THIS MONTH

Remember To Embrace Yourself, In Humility And Victories!

THIS MONTH WAS...

- [ ]
- [ ]
- [ ]
- [ ]
- [ ]
- [ ]
- [ ]
- [ ]
- [ ]

TAKEAWAY

MONTH: _____

AIM FOR
THIS HALF

YEAR: _____

AIM FOR
THIS HALF

> *Success Is Not Measured By The Accolades You Receive, But By The Lives You Impact.*

WEEKLY LIST

INTENTION FOR THE WEEK OF:
_____

MONDAY

TUESDAY

WEDNESDAY

THURSDAY

FRIDAY

SATURDAY

SUNDAY

PRIORITIES

TO DO LIST

WEK | | | |

PRIORITIES

- [ ] _____
- [ ] _____
- [ ] _____

TASKS

- [ ] _____
- [ ] _____
- [ ] _____
- [ ] _____
- [ ] _____
- [ ] _____
- [ ] _____
- [ ] _____

SELF CARE

- [ ] _____
- [ ] _____
- [ ] _____

Affirmation Of The Week

I Am Proud Of The Progress I Made In Prioritizing My Well-being And Self-care This Week.

TAKEAWAY

WEEKLY LIST

INTENTION FOR THE WEEK OF:
_____

MONDAY	TUESDAY

WEDNESDAY	THURSDAY

FRIDAY	SATURDAY
	SUNDAY

PRIORITIES

_____
_____
_____
_____
_____
_____
_____
_____
_____
_____
_____
_____
_____
_____
_____
_____
_____
_____
_____
_____
_____
_____
_____
_____
_____

TO DO LIST

WEK | | | |

PRIORITIES

- [ ] _____
- [ ] _____
- [ ] _____

TASKS

- [ ] _____
- [ ] _____
- [ ] _____
- [ ] _____
- [ ] _____
- [ ] _____
- [ ] _____
- [ ] _____

SELF CARE

- [ ] _____
- [ ] _____
- [ ] _____

Affirmation Of The Week

I Release Any Unfinished Tasks Or Lingering Stress From This Week And Look Forward To A Fresh Start.

TAKEAWAY

WEEKLY LIST

INTENTION FOR THE WEEK OF:
_____

MONDAY

TUESDAY

WEDNESDAY

THURSDAY

FRIDAY

SATURDAY

SUNDAY

PRIORITIES

TO DO LIST

WEK | | |

PRIORITIES

- [ ] _____
- [ ] _____
- [ ] _____

TASKS

- [ ] _____
- [ ] _____
- [ ] _____
- [ ] _____
- [ ] _____
- [ ] _____
- [ ] _____
- [ ] _____

SELF CARE

- [ ] _____
- [ ] _____
- [ ] _____

Affirmation Of The Week

I Am Surrounded By Positivity, Abundance, And Limitless Potential.

TAKEAWAY

WEEKLY LIST

INTENTION FOR THE WEEK OF:
_____

MONDAY

TUESDAY

PRIORITIES

WEDNESDAY

THURSDAY

FRIDAY

SATURDAY

SUNDAY

TO DO LIST

WEEK | | |

PRIORITIES

- [ ] _____
- [ ] _____
- [ ] _____

TASKS

- [ ] _____
- [ ] _____
- [ ] _____
- [ ] _____
- [ ] _____
- [ ] _____
- [ ] _____
- [ ] _____

SELF CARE

- [ ] _____
- [ ] _____
- [ ] _____

Affirmation Of The Week

I Acknowledge And Celebrate My Resilience And Perseverance Throughout This Week.

TAKEAWAY

HABIT TRACKER

HABIT:
_____

TAKEAWAY

- ☐ _____
- ☐ _____
- ☐ _____
- ☐ _____

MONTHLY CHECK IN

I WAS AUTHENTIC THIS MONTH

I WAS CONFIDENT THIS MONTH

I WAS HUMBLE THIS MONTH

I WAS MY BEST THIS MONTH

Remember To Embrace Yourself, In Humility And Victories!

THIS MONTH WAS...

- [ ] _____
- [ ] _____
- [ ] _____
- [ ] _____
- [ ] _____
- [ ] _____
- [ ] _____
- [ ] _____
- [ ] _____

TAKEAWAY

MONTH: _____

AIM FOR
THIS HALF

YEAR: _____

AIM FOR
THIS HALF

> *Your Dedication And Perseverance Are The Keys That Unlock The Doors To Success.*

WEEKLY LIST

INTENTION FOR THE WEEK OF:
_____

MONDAY

TUESDAY

WEDNESDAY

THURSDAY

FRIDAY

SATURDAY

SUNDAY

PRIORITIES

_____
_____
_____
_____
_____
_____
_____
_____
_____
_____
_____
_____
_____
_____
_____
_____
_____
_____
_____
_____
_____
_____
_____
_____
_____
_____
_____

TO DO LIST

WEEK | | | |

PRIORITIES

- [ ] _____
- [ ] _____
- [ ] _____

TASKS

- [ ] _____
- [ ] _____
- [ ] _____
- [ ] _____
- [ ] _____
- [ ] _____
- [ ] _____
- [ ] _____

SELF CARE

- [ ] _____
- [ ] _____
- [ ] _____

Affirmation Of The Week

I Am Open To New Opportunities And Possibilities That Will Come My Way Next Week.

TAKEAWAY

WEEKLY LIST

INTENTION FOR THE WEEK OF:
_____

MONDAY

TUESDAY

WEDNESDAY

THURSDAY

FRIDAY

SATURDAY

SUNDAY

PRIORITIES

_____
_____
_____
_____
_____
_____
_____
_____
_____
_____
_____
_____
_____
_____
_____
_____
_____
_____
_____
_____
_____
_____
_____
_____
_____
_____
_____

TO DO LIST

WEEK | | | |

PRIORITIES

- [ ] _____
- [ ] _____
- [ ] _____

TASKS

- [ ] _____
- [ ] _____
- [ ] _____
- [ ] _____
- [ ] _____
- [ ] _____
- [ ] _____
- [ ] _____

SELF CARE

- [ ] _____
- [ ] _____
- [ ] _____

Affirmation Of The Week

I Choose To Focus On The Good And Positive Moments That Brought Joy To My Week.

TAKEAWAY

WEEKLY LIST

INTENTION FOR THE WEEK OF:
_____

MONDAY

TUESDAY

WEDNESDAY

THURSDAY

FRIDAY

SATURDAY

SUNDAY

PRIORITIES

TO DO LIST

WEEK | | |

PRIORITIES

- [ ] _____
- [ ] _____
- [ ] _____

TASKS

- [ ] _____
- [ ] _____
- [ ] _____
- [ ] _____
- [ ] _____
- [ ] _____
- [ ] _____
- [ ] _____

SELF CARE

- [ ] _____
- [ ] _____
- [ ] _____

Affirmation Of The Week

I Trust In My Ability To Navigate Any Uncertainties That Lie Ahead.

TAKEAWAY

WEEKLY LIST

INTENTION FOR THE WEEK OF:
_____

MONDAY

TUESDAY

WEDNESDAY

THURSDAY

FRIDAY

SATURDAY

SUNDAY

PRIORITIES

_____
_____
_____
_____
_____
_____
_____
_____
_____
_____
_____
_____
_____
_____
_____
_____
_____
_____
_____
_____
_____
_____
_____

TO DO LIST

WEEK | | |

PRIORITIES

- [ ] _____
- [ ] _____
- [ ] _____

TASKS

- [ ] _____
- [ ] _____
- [ ] _____
- [ ] _____
- [ ] _____
- [ ] _____
- [ ] _____
- [ ] _____

SELF CARE

- [ ] _____
- [ ] _____
- [ ] _____

Affirmation Of The Week

I Am Proud Of The Growth And Progress I Made In Both My Personal And Professional Life This Week.

TAKEAWAY

HABIT TRACKER

HABIT:
_____

TAKEAWAY

☐ _____
☐ _____
☐ _____
☐ _____

MONTHLY CHECK IN

I WAS AUTHENTIC THIS MONTH

I WAS CONFIDENT THIS MONTH

I WAS HUMBLE THIS MONTH

I WAS MY BEST THIS MONTH

Remember To Embrace Yourself, In Humility And Victories!

THIS MONTH WAS...

- [ ]
- [ ]
- [ ]
- [ ]
- [ ]
- [ ]
- [ ]
- [ ]
- [ ]

TAKEAWAY

MONTH: _____

AIM FOR
THIS HALF

YEAR: _____

AIM FOR THIS HALF

> *Believe In Your Dreams, For They Hold The Power To Transform Your Reality.*

WEEKLY LIST

INTENTION FOR THE WEEK OF:
_____

MONDAY	TUESDAY

WEDNESDAY	THURSDAY

FRIDAY	SATURDAY
	SUNDAY

PRIORITIES

_____
_____
_____
_____
_____
_____
_____
_____
_____
_____
_____
_____
_____
_____
_____
_____
_____
_____
_____
_____
_____
_____
_____

TO DO LIST

WEK | | | |

PRIORITIES

- [ ] _____
- [ ] _____
- [ ] _____

TASKS

- [ ] _____
- [ ] _____
- [ ] _____
- [ ] _____
- [ ] _____
- [ ] _____
- [ ] _____
- [ ] _____

SELF CARE

- [ ] _____
- [ ] _____
- [ ] _____

Affirmation Of The Week

I Release Any Comparison To Others And Embrace My Unique Journey And Progress.

TAKEAWAY

WEEKLY LIST

INTENTION FOR THE WEEK OF:
_____

MONDAY

TUESDAY

WEDNESDAY

THURSDAY

FRIDAY

SATURDAY

SUNDAY

PRIORITIES

_____
_____
_____
_____
_____
_____
_____
_____
_____
_____
_____
_____
_____
_____
_____
_____
_____
_____
_____
_____
_____
_____
_____
_____

TO DO LIST

WEEK | | | |

PRIORITIES

- [ ] _____
- [ ] _____
- [ ] _____

TASKS

- [ ] _____
- [ ] _____
- [ ] _____
- [ ] _____
- [ ] _____
- [ ] _____
- [ ] _____
- [ ] _____

SELF CARE

- [ ] _____
- [ ] _____
- [ ] _____

Affirmation Of The Week

I Am Open To Receive The Lessons And Blessings That The Next Week Will Bring.

TAKEAWAY

WEEKLY LIST

INTENTION FOR THE WEEK OF:
_____

MONDAY

TUESDAY

WEDNESDAY

THURSDAY

FRIDAY

SATURDAY

SUNDAY

PRIORITIES

TO DO LIST

WEEK | | |

PRIORITIES

- [ ] _____
- [ ] _____
- [ ] _____

TASKS

- [ ] _____
- [ ] _____
- [ ] _____
- [ ] _____
- [ ] _____
- [ ] _____
- [ ] _____
- [ ] _____

SELF CARE

- [ ] _____
- [ ] _____
- [ ] _____

Affirmation Of The Week

I Am Grateful For The Moments Of Self-reflection And Self-discovery That Occurred This Week.

TAKEAWAY

WEEKLY LIST

INTENTION FOR THE WEEK OF: _____

MONDAY	TUESDAY

WEDNESDAY	THURSDAY

FRIDAY	SATURDAY
	SUNDAY

PRIORITIES

_____
_____
_____
_____
_____
_____
_____
_____
_____
_____
_____
_____
_____
_____
_____
_____
_____
_____
_____
_____
_____
_____
_____
_____
_____

TO DO LIST

WEEK | | |

PRIORITIES

- [ ] _____
- [ ] _____
- [ ] _____

TASKS

- [ ] _____
- [ ] _____
- [ ] _____
- [ ] _____
- [ ] _____
- [ ] _____
- [ ] _____
- [ ] _____

SELF CARE

- [ ] _____
- [ ] _____
- [ ] _____

Affirmation Of The Week

I Choose To Let Go Of Any Mistakes Or Regrets From This Week And Embrace Forgiveness And Self-acceptance.

TAKEAWAY

HABIT TRACKER

HABIT:
_____

TAKEAWAY

- ☐ _____
- ☐ _____
- ☐ _____
- ☐ _____

MONTHLY CHECK IN

I WAS AUTHENTIC THIS MONTH

I WAS CONFIDENT THIS MONTH

I WAS HUMBLE THIS MONTH

I WAS MY BEST THIS MONTH

Remember To Embrace Yourself, In Humility And Victories!

THIS MONTH WAS...

- [ ] _____
- [ ] _____
- [ ] _____
- [ ] _____
- [ ] _____
- [ ] _____
- [ ] _____
- [ ] _____
- [ ] _____

TAKEAWAY

MONTH: _____

AIM FOR
THIS HALF

YEAR: _____

AIM FOR
THIS HALF

> *Your Goals Are The Lighthouses That Guide You Through The Stormy Seas Of Life.*

WEEKLY LIST

INTENTION FOR THE WEEK OF:
_____

MONDAY

TUESDAY

PRIORITIES

WEDNESDAY

THURSDAY

FRIDAY

SATURDAY

SUNDAY

TO DO LIST

WEEK | | | |

PRIORITIES

- [ ] _____
- [ ] _____
- [ ] _____

TASKS

- [ ] _____
- [ ] _____
- [ ] _____
- [ ] _____
- [ ] _____
- [ ] _____
- [ ] _____
- [ ] _____

SELF CARE

- [ ] _____
- [ ] _____
- [ ] _____

Affirmation Of The Week

I Am Worthy Of Success, Happiness, And Abundance In All Areas Of My Life.

TAKEAWAY

WEEKLY LIST

INTENTION FOR THE WEEK OF:
_____

MONDAY

TUESDAY

PRIORITIES

_____
_____
_____
_____
_____
_____
_____
_____

WEDNESDAY

THURSDAY

_____
_____
_____
_____
_____
_____
_____
_____
_____
_____
_____
_____

FRIDAY

SATURDAY

_____
_____
_____
_____
_____

SUNDAY

_____
_____
_____

TO DO LIST

WEEK | | |

PRIORITIES

- [ ] _____
- [ ] _____
- [ ] _____

TASKS

- [ ] _____
- [ ] _____
- [ ] _____
- [ ] _____
- [ ] _____
- [ ] _____
- [ ] _____
- [ ] _____

SELF CARE

- [ ] _____
- [ ] _____
- [ ] _____

Affirmation Of The Week

I Acknowledge And Celebrate My Efforts And Commitment To My Goals This Week.

TAKEAWAY

WEEKLY LIST

INTENTION FOR THE WEEK OF:
_____

MONDAY	TUESDAY
WEDNESDAY	THURSDAY
FRIDAY	SATURDAY
	SUNDAY

PRIORITIES

_____
_____
_____
_____
_____
_____
_____
_____
_____
_____
_____
_____
_____
_____
_____
_____
_____
_____
_____
_____
_____
_____
_____

TO DO LIST

WEEK | | |

PRIORITIES

- [ ] _____
- [ ] _____
- [ ] _____

TASKS

- [ ] _____
- [ ] _____
- [ ] _____
- [ ] _____
- [ ] _____
- [ ] _____
- [ ] _____
- [ ] _____

SELF CARE

- [ ] _____
- [ ] _____
- [ ] _____

Affirmation Of The Week

I Release Any Worries Or Anxieties About The Future And Trust In The Unfolding Of My Path.

TAKEAWAY

WEEKLY LIST

INTENTION FOR THE WEEK OF:
_____

MONDAY

TUESDAY

WEDNESDAY

THURSDAY

FRIDAY

SATURDAY

SUNDAY

PRIORITIES

_____
_____
_____
_____
_____
_____
_____
_____
_____
_____
_____
_____
_____
_____
_____
_____
_____
_____
_____
_____
_____
_____

TO DO LIST

WEEK | | |

PRIORITIES

- [ ] _____
- [ ] _____
- [ ] _____

TASKS

- [ ] _____
- [ ] _____
- [ ] _____
- [ ] _____
- [ ] _____
- [ ] _____
- [ ] _____
- [ ] _____

SELF CARE

- [ ] _____
- [ ] _____
- [ ] _____

Affirmation Of The Week

I Am Surrounded By Love, Positivity, And Supportive Energies.

TAKEAWAY

HABIT TRACKER

HABIT:
_____

TAKEAWAY

☐ _____
☐ _____
☐ _____
☐ _____

MONTHLY CHECK IN

I WAS AUTHENTIC THIS MONTH

I WAS CONFIDENT THIS MONTH

I WAS HUMBLE THIS MONTH

I WAS MY BEST THIS MONTH

Remember To Embrace Yourself, In Humility And Victories!

THIS MONTH WAS...

- [ ] _____
- [ ] _____
- [ ] _____
- [ ] _____
- [ ] _____
- [ ] _____
- [ ] _____
- [ ] _____
- [ ] _____

TAKEAWAY

MONTH: _____

AIM FOR
THIS HALF

YEAR: _____

AIM FOR THIS HALF

> *Your Passion Is The Fuel That Ignites Your Dreams And Propels You Towards Greatness.*

WEEKLY LIST

INTENTION FOR THE WEEK OF:
_____

MONDAY	TUESDAY

WEDNESDAY	THURSDAY

FRIDAY	SATURDAY
	SUNDAY

PRIORITIES

_____
_____
_____
_____
_____
_____
_____
_____
_____
_____
_____
_____
_____
_____
_____
_____
_____
_____
_____
_____
_____
_____
_____
_____
_____
_____

TO DO LIST

WEEK | | |

PRIORITIES

- [ ] _____
- [ ] _____
- [ ] _____

TASKS

- [ ] _____
- [ ] _____
- [ ] _____
- [ ] _____
- [ ] _____
- [ ] _____
- [ ] _____
- [ ] _____

SELF CARE

- [ ] _____
- [ ] _____
- [ ] _____

Affirmation Of The Week

I Choose To Focus On My Strengths And Achievements Rather Than Dwelling On Any Perceived Shortcomings.

TAKEAWAY

WEEKLY LIST

INTENTION FOR THE WEEK OF:
_____

MONDAY

TUESDAY

WEDNESDAY

THURSDAY

FRIDAY

SATURDAY

SUNDAY

PRIORITIES

TO DO LIST

WEEK | | |

PRIORITIES

- [ ] _____
- [ ] _____
- [ ] _____

TASKS

- [ ] _____
- [ ] _____
- [ ] _____
- [ ] _____
- [ ] _____
- [ ] _____
- [ ] _____
- [ ] _____

SELF CARE

- [ ] _____
- [ ] _____
- [ ] _____

Affirmation Of The Week

I Am Grateful For The Connections And Relationships That Brought Joy And Fulfillment To My Week.

TAKEAWAY

WEEKLY LIST

INTENTION FOR THE WEEK OF:
_____

MONDAY

TUESDAY

WEDNESDAY

THURSDAY

FRIDAY

SATURDAY

SUNDAY

PRIORITIES

_____
_____
_____
_____
_____
_____
_____
_____
_____
_____
_____
_____
_____
_____
_____
_____
_____
_____
_____
_____
_____
_____
_____
_____
_____

TO DO LIST

WEK | | | |

PRIORITIES

- [ ] _____
- [ ] _____
- [ ] _____

TASKS

- [ ] _____
- [ ] _____
- [ ] _____
- [ ] _____
- [ ] _____
- [ ] _____
- [ ] _____
- [ ] _____

SELF CARE

- [ ] _____
- [ ] _____
- [ ] _____

Affirmation Of The Week

I am excited about the opportunities for growth and learning that await me in the upcoming week.

TAKEAWAY

WEEKLY LIST

INTENTION FOR THE WEEK OF:
_____

MONDAY

TUESDAY

WEDNESDAY

THURSDAY

FRIDAY

SATURDAY

SUNDAY

PRIORITIES

_____
_____
_____
_____
_____
_____
_____
_____
_____
_____
_____
_____
_____
_____
_____
_____
_____
_____
_____
_____
_____
_____
_____

TO DO LIST

WEEK | | |

PRIORITIES

- [ ] _____
- [ ] _____
- [ ] _____

TASKS

- [ ] _____
- [ ] _____
- [ ] _____
- [ ] _____
- [ ] _____
- [ ] _____
- [ ] _____
- [ ] _____

SELF CARE

- [ ] _____
- [ ] _____
- [ ] _____

Affirmation Of The Week

I Embrace The Power Of Positivity And Optimism As I Transition Into The Next Week.

TAKEAWAY

HABIT TRACKER

HABIT:
_____

TAKEAWAY

☐ _____
☐ _____
☐ _____
☐ _____

MONTHLY CHECK IN

I WAS AUTHENTIC THIS MONTH

I WAS CONFIDENT THIS MONTH

I WAS HUMBLE THIS MONTH

I WAS MY BEST THIS MONTH

Remember To Embrace Yourself, In Humility And Victories!

THIS MONTH WAS...

- [ ]
- [ ]
- [ ]
- [ ]
- [ ]
- [ ]
- [ ]
- [ ]
- [ ]

TAKEAWAY

MONTH: _____

AIM FOR
THIS HALF

YEAR: _____

AIM FOR THIS HALF

> *Your Purpose Is Not Just A Destination But A Guiding Light That Illuminates Your Path.*

WEEKLY LIST

INTENTION FOR THE WEEK OF:
_____

MONDAY

TUESDAY

WEDNESDAY

THURSDAY

FRIDAY

SATURDAY

SUNDAY

PRIORITIES

_____
_____
_____
_____
_____
_____
_____
_____
_____
_____
_____
_____
_____
_____
_____
_____
_____
_____
_____
_____
_____
_____
_____

TO DO LIST

WEEK | | |

PRIORITIES

- [ ] _____
- [ ] _____
- [ ] _____

TASKS

- [ ] _____
- [ ] _____
- [ ] _____
- [ ] _____
- [ ] _____
- [ ] _____
- [ ] _____
- [ ] _____

SELF CARE

- [ ] _____
- [ ] _____
- [ ] _____

Affirmation Of The Week

I Am Proud Of Myself For Staying True To My Values And Integrity Throughout This Week.

TAKEAWAY

WEEKLY LIST

INTENTION FOR THE WEEK OF _____

MONDAY	TUESDAY

WEDNESDAY	THURSDAY

FRIDAY	SATURDAY
	SUNDAY

PRIORITIES

_____
_____
_____
_____
_____
_____
_____
_____
_____
_____
_____
_____
_____
_____
_____
_____
_____
_____
_____
_____
_____
_____
_____
_____
_____

TO DO LIST

WEK | | | |

PRIORITIES

- [ ] _____
- [ ] _____
- [ ] _____

TASKS

- [ ] _____
- [ ] _____
- [ ] _____
- [ ] _____
- [ ] _____
- [ ] _____
- [ ] _____
- [ ] _____

SELF CARE

- [ ] _____
- [ ] _____
- [ ] _____

Affirmation Of The Week

I Release Any Expectations Or Pressures And Embrace The Freedom To Simply Be Myself.

TAKEAWAY

WEEKLY LIST

INTENTION FOR THE WEEK OF:
_____

MONDAY

TUESDAY

WEDNESDAY

THURSDAY

FRIDAY

SATURDAY

SUNDAY

PRIORITIES

_____
_____
_____
_____
_____
_____
_____
_____
_____
_____
_____
_____
_____
_____
_____
_____
_____
_____
_____
_____
_____
_____
_____
_____

TO DO LIST

WEEK | | |

PRIORITIES

- [ ] _____
- [ ] _____
- [ ] _____

TASKS

- [ ] _____
- [ ] _____
- [ ] _____
- [ ] _____
- [ ] _____
- [ ] _____
- [ ] _____
- [ ] _____

SELF CARE

- [ ] _____
- [ ] _____
- [ ] _____

Affirmation Of The Week

I Am Open To Receive Guidance, Inspiration, And Intuitive Insights In The Next Week.

TAKEAWAY

WEEKLY LIST

INTENTION FOR THE WEEK OF:
_____

MONDAY

TUESDAY

PRIORITIES

_____
_____
_____
_____
_____
_____
_____
_____
_____
_____

WEDNESDAY

THURSDAY

_____
_____
_____
_____
_____
_____
_____
_____
_____
_____

FRIDAY

SATURDAY

_____
_____
_____
_____
_____

SUNDAY

_____
_____
_____

TO DO LIST

WEEK | | |

PRIORITIES

- [ ] _____
- [ ] _____
- [ ] _____

TASKS

- [ ] _____
- [ ] _____
- [ ] _____
- [ ] _____
- [ ] _____
- [ ] _____
- [ ] _____
- [ ] _____

SELF CARE

- [ ] _____
- [ ] _____
- [ ] _____

Affirmation Of The Week

I Celebrate My Unique Journey And Progress, Knowing That Comparison Has No Place In My Life.

TAKEAWAY

HABIT TRACKER

HABIT:
_____

TAKEAWAY

- ☐ _____
- ☐ _____
- ☐ _____
- ☐ _____

MONTHLY CHECK IN

I WAS AUTHENTIC THIS MONTH

I WAS CONFIDENT THIS MONTH

I WAS HUMBLE THIS MONTH

I WAS MY BEST THIS MONTH

Remember To Embrace Yourself, In Humility And Victories!

THIS MONTH WAS...

- [ ] _____
- [ ] _____
- [ ] _____
- [ ] _____
- [ ] _____
- [ ] _____
- [ ] _____
- [ ] _____
- [ ] _____

TAKEAWAY

MONTH: _____

AIM FOR
THIS HALF

YEAR: _____

AIM FOR THIS HALF

> *Your Dreams Are The Seeds Of Greatness. Nurture Them With Unwavering Belief And Relentless Action.*

WEEKLY LIST

INTENTION FOR THE WEEK OF:
_____

MONDAY

TUESDAY

PRIORITIES

_____
_____
_____
_____
_____
_____
_____
_____
_____
_____
_____
_____
_____
_____
_____
_____
_____
_____
_____
_____
_____
_____

WEDNESDAY

THURSDAY

FRIDAY

SATURDAY

SUNDAY

TO DO LIST

WEEK | | |

PRIORITIES

- [ ] _____
- [ ] _____
- [ ] _____

TASKS

- [ ] _____
- [ ] _____
- [ ] _____
- [ ] _____
- [ ] _____
- [ ] _____
- [ ] _____
- [ ] _____

SELF CARE

- [ ] _____
- [ ] _____
- [ ] _____

Affirmation Of The Week

I Am Grateful For The Moments Of Joy, Laughter, And Happiness That Brightened My Week.

TAKEAWAY

WEEKLY LIST

INTENTION FOR THE WEEK OF:
_____

MONDAY	TUESDAY

WEDNESDAY	THURSDAY

FRIDAY	SATURDAY
	SUNDAY

PRIORITIES

_____
_____
_____
_____
_____
_____
_____
_____
_____
_____
_____
_____
_____
_____
_____
_____
_____
_____
_____
_____
_____
_____
_____

TO DO LIST

WEK | | | |

PRIORITIES

- [ ] _____
- [ ] _____
- [ ] _____

TASKS

- [ ] _____
- [ ] _____
- [ ] _____
- [ ] _____
- [ ] _____
- [ ] _____
- [ ] _____
- [ ] _____

SELF CARE

- [ ] _____
- [ ] _____
- [ ] _____

Affirmation Of The Week

I Choose To See Setbacks As Opportunities For Growth And Redirection Towards My Goals.

TAKEAWAY

WEEKLY LIST

INTENTION FOR THE WEEK OF:
_____

MONDAY

TUESDAY

WEDNESDAY

THURSDAY

FRIDAY

SATURDAY

SUNDAY

PRIORITIES

_____
_____
_____
_____
_____
_____
_____
_____
_____
_____
_____
_____
_____
_____
_____
_____
_____
_____
_____
_____
_____
_____
_____
_____
_____
_____

TO DO LIST

WEEK | | |

PRIORITIES

- [ ] _____
- [ ] _____
- [ ] _____

TASKS

- [ ] _____
- [ ] _____
- [ ] _____
- [ ] _____
- [ ] _____
- [ ] _____
- [ ] _____
- [ ] _____

SELF CARE

- [ ] _____
- [ ] _____
- [ ] _____

Affirmation Of The Week

I Am Excited About The Possibilities And New Beginnings That The Next Week Holds For Me.

TAKEAWAY

WEEKLY LIST

INTENTION FOR THE WEEK OF: _____

MONDAY

TUESDAY

WEDNESDAY

THURSDAY

FRIDAY

SATURDAY

SUNDAY

PRIORITIES

_____
_____
_____
_____
_____
_____
_____
_____
_____
_____
_____
_____
_____
_____
_____
_____
_____
_____
_____
_____
_____
_____
_____
_____
_____
_____
_____
_____

TO DO LIST

WEEK | | |

PRIORITIES

- [ ] _____
- [ ] _____
- [ ] _____

TASKS

- [ ] _____
- [ ] _____
- [ ] _____
- [ ] _____
- [ ] _____
- [ ] _____
- [ ] _____
- [ ] _____

SELF CARE

- [ ] _____
- [ ] _____
- [ ] _____

Affirmation Of The Week

I Acknowledge And Appreciate The Effort And Dedication I Put Into My Work And Projects This Week.

TAKEAWAY

HABIT TRACKER

HABIT:
_____

TAKEAWAY

- ☐ _____
- ☐ _____
- ☐ _____
- ☐ _____

MONTHLY CHECK IN

I WAS AUTHENTIC THIS MONTH

I WAS CONFIDENT THIS MONTH

I WAS HUMBLE THIS MONTH

I WAS MY BEST THIS MONTH

Remember To Embrace Yourself, In Humility And Victories!

THIS MONTH WAS...

- [ ] _____
- [ ] _____
- [ ] _____
- [ ] _____
- [ ] _____
- [ ] _____
- [ ] _____
- [ ] _____
- [ ] _____

TAKEAWAY

MONTH: _____

AIM FOR
THIS HALF

YEAR: _____

AIM FOR THIS HALF

> *Let Your Actions Be Guided By Intention And Purpose, And Watch Miracles Manifest.*

WEEKLY LIST

INTENTION FOR THE WEEK OF:
_____

MONDAY

TUESDAY

PRIORITIES

_____
_____
_____
_____
_____
_____
_____
_____
_____
_____
_____
_____
_____
_____
_____
_____
_____
_____
_____
_____
_____
_____
_____
_____

WEDNESDAY

THURSDAY

FRIDAY

SATURDAY

SUNDAY

TO DO LIST

WEEK | | |

PRIORITIES

- [ ] _____
- [ ] _____
- [ ] _____

TASKS

- [ ] _____
- [ ] _____
- [ ] _____
- [ ] _____
- [ ] _____
- [ ] _____
- [ ] _____
- [ ] _____

SELF CARE

- [ ] _____
- [ ] _____
- [ ] _____

Affirmation Of The Week

I Release Any Fears Or Doubts And Trust In The Universe's Plan For My Life.

TAKEAWAY

WEEKLY LIST

INTENTION FOR THE WEEK OF:
_____

MONDAY

TUESDAY

WEDNESDAY

THURSDAY

FRIDAY

SATURDAY

SUNDAY

PRIORITIES

_____
_____
_____
_____
_____
_____
_____
_____
_____
_____
_____
_____
_____
_____
_____
_____
_____
_____
_____
_____
_____
_____
_____
_____

TO DO LIST

WEEK | | |

PRIORITIES

- [ ] _____
- [ ] _____
- [ ] _____

TASKS

- [ ] _____
- [ ] _____
- [ ] _____
- [ ] _____
- [ ] _____
- [ ] _____
- [ ] _____
- [ ] _____

SELF CARE

- [ ] _____
- [ ] _____
- [ ] _____

Affirmation Of The Week

I Am Grateful For The Experiences That Brought Me Closer To My Dreams And Aspirations This Week.

TAKEAWAY

WEEKLY LIST

INTENTION FOR THE WEEK OF:
_____

MONDAY

TUESDAY

WEDNESDAY

THURSDAY

FRIDAY

SATURDAY

SUNDAY

PRIORITIES

TO DO LIST

WEEK | | |

PRIORITIES

- [ ] _____
- [ ] _____
- [ ] _____

TASKS

- [ ] _____
- [ ] _____
- [ ] _____
- [ ] _____
- [ ] _____
- [ ] _____
- [ ] _____
- [ ] _____

SELF CARE

- [ ] _____
- [ ] _____
- [ ] _____

Affirmation Of The Week

I Am Open To Receiving Abundance, Success, And Fulfillment In The Upcoming Week.

TAKEAWAY

WEEKLY LIST

INTENTION FOR THE WEEK OF:
_____

MONDAY

TUESDAY

WEDNESDAY

THURSDAY

FRIDAY

SATURDAY

SUNDAY

PRIORITIES

_____
_____
_____
_____
_____
_____
_____
_____
_____
_____
_____
_____
_____
_____
_____
_____
_____
_____
_____
_____
_____
_____
_____
_____
_____
_____
_____

TO DO LIST

WEEK | | |

PRIORITIES

- [ ] _____
- [ ] _____
- [ ] _____

TASKS

- [ ] _____
- [ ] _____
- [ ] _____
- [ ] _____
- [ ] _____
- [ ] _____
- [ ] _____
- [ ] _____

SELF CARE

- [ ] _____
- [ ] _____
- [ ] _____

Affirmation Of The Week

I Celebrate The Moments Of Self-care And Self-nurturing That I Prioritized This Week.

TAKEAWAY

HABIT TRACKER

HABIT:
_____

TAKEAWAY

- ☐ _____
- ☐ _____
- ☐ _____
- ☐ _____

MONTHLY CHECK IN

I WAS AUTHENTIC THIS MONTH

I WAS CONFIDENT THIS MONTH

I WAS HUMBLE THIS MONTH

I WAS MY BEST THIS MONTH

Remember To Embrace Yourself, In Humility And Victories!

THIS MONTH WAS...

- [ ] _____
- [ ] _____
- [ ] _____
- [ ] _____
- [ ] _____
- [ ] _____
- [ ] _____
- [ ] _____
- [ ] _____

TAKEAWAY

MONTH: _____

AIM FOR
THIS HALF

YEAR: _____

AIM FOR THIS HALF

> *Seize The Day, For It Holds The Key To Unlock The Doors Of Opportunity And Transformation.*

WEEKLY LIST

INTENTION FOR THE WEEK OF:
_____

MONDAY

TUESDAY

WEDNESDAY

THURSDAY

FRIDAY

SATURDAY

SUNDAY

PRIORITIES

_____
_____
_____
_____
_____
_____
_____
_____
_____
_____
_____
_____
_____
_____
_____
_____
_____
_____
_____
_____
_____
_____

TO DO LIST

WEK | | | |

PRIORITIES

- [ ] _____
- [ ] _____
- [ ] _____

TASKS

- [ ] _____
- [ ] _____
- [ ] _____
- [ ] _____
- [ ] _____
- [ ] _____
- [ ] _____
- [ ] _____

SELF CARE

- [ ] _____
- [ ] _____
- [ ] _____

Affirmation Of The Week

I Choose To Focus On The Positive Impact I Made On Others' Lives Throughout This Week.

TAKEAWAY

WEEKLY LIST

INTENTION FOR THE WEEK OF:
_____

MONDAY

TUESDAY

WEDNESDAY

THURSDAY

FRIDAY

SATURDAY

SUNDAY

PRIORITIES

_____
_____
_____
_____
_____
_____
_____
_____
_____
_____
_____
_____
_____
_____
_____
_____
_____
_____
_____
_____
_____
_____

TO DO LIST

WEEK | | |

PRIORITIES

- [ ] _____
- [ ] _____
- [ ] _____

TASKS

- [ ] _____
- [ ] _____
- [ ] _____
- [ ] _____
- [ ] _____
- [ ] _____
- [ ] _____
- [ ] _____

SELF CARE

- [ ] _____
- [ ] _____
- [ ] _____

Affirmation Of The Week

I Am Grateful For The Valuable Lessons And Insights Gained From My Experiences This Week.

TAKEAWAY

WEEKLY LIST

INTENTION FOR THE WEEK OF:
_____

MONDAY

TUESDAY

WEDNESDAY

THURSDAY

FRIDAY

SATURDAY

SUNDAY

PRIORITIES

_____
_____
_____
_____
_____
_____
_____
_____
_____
_____
_____
_____
_____
_____
_____
_____
_____
_____
_____
_____
_____
_____
_____
_____

TO DO LIST

WEEK | | |

PRIORITIES

- [ ] _____
- [ ] _____
- [ ] _____

TASKS

- [ ] _____
- [ ] _____
- [ ] _____
- [ ] _____
- [ ] _____
- [ ] _____
- [ ] _____
- [ ] _____

SELF CARE

- [ ] _____
- [ ] _____
- [ ] _____

Affirmation Of The Week

I Release Any Negative Self-talk Or Limiting Beliefs And Embrace Self-empowerment And Positivity.

TAKEAWAY

WEEKLY LIST

INTENTION FOR THE WEEK OF:
_____

MONDAY	TUESDAY

WEDNESDAY	THURSDAY

FRIDAY	SATURDAY
	SUNDAY

PRIORITIES

_____
_____
_____
_____
_____
_____
_____
_____
_____
_____
_____
_____
_____
_____
_____
_____
_____
_____
_____
_____
_____
_____
_____
_____

TO DO LIST

WEEK | | |

PRIORITIES

- [ ] _____
- [ ] _____
- [ ] _____

TASKS

- [ ] _____
- [ ] _____
- [ ] _____
- [ ] _____
- [ ] _____
- [ ] _____
- [ ] _____
- [ ] _____

SELF CARE

- [ ] _____
- [ ] _____
- [ ] _____

Affirmation Of The Week

I Am Proud Of Myself For Showing Up, Staying Committed, And Giving My Best Throughout This Week.

TAKEAWAY

HABIT TRACKER

HABIT:
_____

TAKEAWAY

☐ _____
☐ _____
☐ _____
☐ _____

MONTHLY CHECK IN

I WAS AUTHENTIC THIS MONTH

I WAS CONFIDENT THIS MONTH

I WAS HUMBLE THIS MONTH

I WAS MY BEST THIS MONTH

Remember To Embrace Yourself, In Humility And Victories!

THIS MONTH WAS...

- [ ] _____
- [ ] _____
- [ ] _____
- [ ] _____
- [ ] _____
- [ ] _____
- [ ] _____
- [ ] _____
- [ ] _____

TAKEAWAY

You Did It! In A World That Often Expects Us To Conform, You Celebrate The Beauty Of Being True To Yourself.

Did You Get To Your Goals?

REFLECTION

- [ ] _____
- [ ] _____
- [ ] _____
- [ ] _____
- [ ] _____
- [ ] _____
- [ ] _____
- [ ] _____
- [ ] _____
- [ ] _____

A Note To Your Self

BE KIND BE GRATEFUL BE HUMBLE BE AUTHENTIC BE CONFIDENT

Thank You!

Thank you for using this space to express your thoughts, dreams, and aspirations without judgment. I hope it proved to be a safe haven where you could explore your passions, set meaningful goals, and embark on a journey of self-empowerment.

Don't stop now, this is just the beginning!

What's Next?

Order your next Daily Success Map to continue your journey.

I can't wait to see what's next for you!

www.ingramcontent.com/pod-product-compliance
Lightning Source LLC
Chambersburg PA
CBHW061406010526
44119CB00011B/272